CONTENTS

CW00446832

CHOICE

Fred D'Aguiar • *Letters to America* • Carcanet Press

RECOMMENDATIONS

Daisy Lafarge • *Life Without Air* • Granta Books
Bill Manhire • *Wow* • Carcanet Press
Nii Ayikwei Parkes • *The Geez* • Peepal Tree Press
Safiya Sinclair • *Cannibal* • Picador

SPECIAL COMMENDATION

Staying Human: New Poems for Staying Alive • Bloodaxe Books

RECOMMENDED TRANSLATIONS

Kiwao Nomura • *The Day Laid Bare* • Isobar Press
Translated by Eric Selland
Maram al-Masri • *The Abduction* • Southword Editions
Translated by Theo Dorgan

PAMPHLET CHOICE

William Gee • *Rheuma* • Bad Betty Press

WILD CARD

Matthew Sweeney • *Shadow of the Owl* • Bloodaxe Books

Poetry Book Society

CHOICE SELECTORS RECOMMENDATION SPECIAL COMMENDATION	SINÉAD MORRISSEY & ANDREW McMILLAN
TRANSLATION SELECTOR	ILYA KAMINSKY
PAMPHLET SELECTORS	MARY JEAN CHAN & NICK MAKOHA
WILD CARD SELECTOR	ANTHONY ANAXAGOROU
CONTRIBUTORS	SOPHIE O'NEILL NATHANIEL SPAIN
EDITORIAL & DESIGN	ALICE KATE MULLEN

Poetry Book Society Memberships

Choice
4 Books a Year: 4 Choice books & 4 *Bulletins* a year (UK £55, Europe £65, ROW £75)

World
8 Books: 4 Choices, 4 Translation books & 4 *Bulletins* (£98, £120, £132)

Charter
20 Books: 4 Choices, 16 Recommendations and 4 *Bulletins* (£180, £210, £235)

Complete
24 Books: 4 Choices, 16 Recommendations, 4 Translations, 4 *Bulletins* (£223, £265, £292)

Single copies of the *Bulletin* £9.99

Cover Art Nana Yaw Oduro, Instagram @the.vintage.mason

Copyright Poetry Book Society and contributors. All rights reserved.
ISBN 9781913129200 ISSN 0551-1690

Poetry Book Society | Milburn House | Dean Street | Newcastle upon Tyne | NE1 1LF
0191 230 8100 | enquiries@poetrybooksociety.co.uk

WWW.POETRYBOOKS.CO.UK

LETTER FROM THE PBS

We have a really tremendous line up of selections in this Winter *Bulletin*; political, prophetic, ecological, thought provoking, moving and truly international. Congratulations to Fred D'Aguiar for receiving the Choice with his hugely topical and personal *Letters to America*. We hope this season we are introducing you to new names in poetry alongside those who are more established.

Sinéad Morrisey says of the brand new *Staying Human* anthology from Bloodaxe: "Buy this book. Buy it for your friends. It's a present to last a lifetime." After reading our poet selector commentaries and poets themselves, we have no doubt you will be lured into wanting every book, so order them quick, while stocks last!

While on the subject of buying for friends, we know this year gifting is going to be a challenge, so let the PBS solve this problem for you with our PBS gift membership. As this turbulent year continues, more and more people have been turning to poetry and we have a good feeling poetry will be *the* gift this Christmas. If every member bought one gift membership it would have a huge impact on the PBS and the careers of the poets we support – all PBS profits go straight back into promoting contemporary poetry and poets. You can purchase easily online, or please give us a call (0191 230 8100) and we can arrange gift membership over the phone.

We are continuing our online series of events and it has been great to see so many of you "digitally". To launch this *Bulletin*, Fred D'Aguiar and David Morley will be reading and in conversation with Selector Sinéad Morrisey at NCLA on 26th November at 7pm on Zoom. Our next insta-bookclub is 7pm on 12th November with the fabulous Nii Ayikwei Parkes alongside selectors Anthony Anaxagorou and Andrew McMillan. Keep a look on our social media and website for more details and full recordings of the events.

Thanks for all your kind messages of support over the past year, we love to hear from you and really appreciate your words which have kept us going in the darker times! If we don't speak to you before December, have a wonderful Christmas and we'll be in touch in the New Year.

SOPHIE O'NEILL
PBS & INPRESS DIRECTOR

FRED D'AGUIAR

Fred D'Aguiar was born in London in 1960 to Guyanese parents. He grew up in Guyana, returning to England in his teens. He trained as a psychiatric nurse before reading English with African and Caribbean Studies at the University of Kent, Canterbury. He was Northern Arts Literary Fellow at Newcastle and Durham Universities, and Judith E. Wilson Fellow at Cambridge University and has been shortlisted twice for the T.S. Eliot Prize. *Letters to America* is his eighth book of poetry. He is also the author of five novels, the first of which, *The Longest Memory* (Chatto, 1994), won both the David Higham Prize for Fiction and the Whitbread First Novel Award. His plays include *High Life* (1987) and *A Jamaican Airman Foresees His Death* (1991), which was performed at the Royal Court Theatre, London. *Mr. Reasonable* was broadcast on BBC Radio 4 in 2015. He is Professor of English at University of California, Los Angeles.

LETTERS TO AMERICA

CARCANET PRESS | £10.99 | PBS PRICE   £8.25

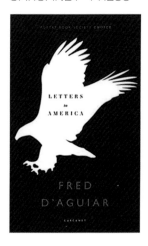

The word "to" in the title of Fred D'Aguiar's new collection is doing a lot of work I think; on one level it's a pun drawn from the eponymous poem's Abecedarian form which closes the collection, but on another, deeper, level, the fact these are letters "to" rather than "from" America mean that we can read many of the poems here as despatches of address, showing back to a nation a series of reflections and vantages of itself, in order that it might begin to rebuild. In poems like 'The Border' and 'Axe' it feels as though D'Aguiar is giving us new fables, new parables through which the nation might better understand its current predicaments and how it arrived at them.

In the afore-mentioned Abecedarian poem, and in several others, there is a glorious reaching and expanse of form, as though the poems are striving to meet the urgency and complexity of the current moment. The long lines of 'Bullet', which seem to whistle through the air to the end of each margin, and chillingly vocalise the projectile as it inflicts death and destruction, are a particular highlight.

> I fly through wood doors, walls, curtain or blind covered windows.
> He is an old man. He knows aerodynamics. He knows a lot about
> me. We are introduced. But it is a meeting he will never remember

In '1960', D'Aguiar's final stanza reads:

> My year petered out like a wet
> Guy Fawkes, left me standing,
> Not with a broken heart, but
> Stuck up to my ankles in data
> From an era where a stranger
> Looks into my pram and tells
> My mother that my red hair
> And brown skin made me a
> Bloody freak of nature.

We have that wonderful simile in the opening lines, and then that rhythm and propulsion created by "data", "stranger" and "nature" all echoing off one another, with "mother" and "era" joining in faintly at the beginning of the 5th and 7th lines. This is just one example of the fine-tuned excellence on display here.

ANDREW McMILLAN

FRED D'AGUIAR

In November 2016 my undergraduate creative writing students at UCLA, shocked by the election results, walked out of class to join a spontaneous demonstration around campus. We were in the middle of a studio-style workshop pouring over a poem (Oh semicolon, you tadpole in a top-hat, are you worthy of inclusion?) when the protest chants flooded the room. Four-beats per line, two-couplets, "1, 2, 3, 4, / we won't listen anymore; / 2, 4, 6, 8, / this election is a fake."

The last of my students to leave the room paused at the door and looked at me. In the half-minute that it took students to file out I weighed the betrayal the young felt: that the liberal political machine (which demanded young people's loyalty and trust) had abnegated its assumed responsibility and paved the way for the most unsound Presidential candidate in living memory to win the White House.

I caught up with the students. They cheered me for joining them. We became the demonstration: a giant snake hissing its way around campus. The buildings and trees amplified our marching chants. I grew giddy and hoarse. Eventually the protestors doubled back to the classroom building. I peeled off and headed inside thinking I'd leave the students to continue demonstrating. But my students followed me. They said that they'd marched enough, that they wanted to continue with class, since I'd joined them in their protest.

For the rest of the workshop we were alert to poetry as affective impulse (a diss to despotic order) grafted to social address. We conjured ways to migrate from private to public, from national to international spheres, and back, even as we kept loyal to the local. Class ran over time; no one wanted to leave the room, though we'd settled the question of semicolons ages ago.

FRED RECOMMENDS

Moniza Alvi, *Europa* (Bloodaxe); André Naffis-Sahely, *The Heart of a Stranger* (Pushkin Press) and *The Promised Land* (Penguin); *Un Nuevo Sol: British Latinx Writers*, ed. Nathalie Teitler and Nii Ayikwei Parkes (Flipped Eye); Natalie Diaz, *Postcolonial Love Poem* (Faber); Sandeep Parmer, *Eidolon* (Shearsman); *I am a Rohingya: Poetry from the Camps and Beyond* (Arc); Grace Nichols, *I Have Crossed an Ocean, Selected Poems* (Bloodaxe); John Agard, *Alternative Anthem* (Bloodaxe); Jay Bernard, *Surge* (Chatto); Vahni Capildeo, *Utter* (Peepal Tree Press); Maura Dooley, *The Silvering* (Bloodaxe); Chris Beckett and Alemu Tebeje, *Songs We Learn From Trees* (Carcanet); Mark Ford, *Six Children* (Faber); Sinéad Morrissey, *On Balance* (Carcanet); Ahren Warner, *Confer* (Bloodaxe); Linda Anderson, *The Station Before* (Pavilion Poetry) and Andrew McMillan, *physical* (Cape).

CHOICE

BLACK LIVES MATTER

brings us to this day on a dead-end street, face-to-face
with a young rabbit, no bigger than a tangerine,

blue jays pick up with articulate claws, fly four floors and drop,
but lucky nine lives rabbit lands, thud, looks hurt,

stays still for seconds, as if lost in dream space,
staggers away, and another jay grabs it, until we intervene,

shoo those blue jays into treetops, and wrap
the pulse of fur, with two dimes for ears, in an old T-shirt.

Too young for us to feed it carrots or lettuce, we know
that we must release the bright bulb of a creature back

where we found it, but not before we chase
those lingering jays, place shirt gingerly on dirt, watch that

fur ball flick away into tall, abandoned, lot grass,
as if that bulb lost its element and left an afterglow.

We wait as jays circle, then tip wings for another zone.
We retrieve that tee, its smell of game, and tiptoe home.

BODY COUNT (EXTRACT)

Turn right out New Cross station
    left onto exhaust fumigated A2
        outpace inching traffic
            dodge a cycling youth
                barreling along the pavement
                  look up at plaque
              down at how far each jumped
            chased by deliberate fire

        bass drives blood
      drum fuels pulse
lightning through brain
      blood writes history
         timed on pulse
            shock waves brain

                if one police in each station says
                    'no more chokeholds on my watch
                no more hearts stopped on my beat'
            how many Black lives will that save?

        Do the math
      add one to one hundred
take away ten black people
      divide that by two enquiries
        what do you have?

Image: Elikem Akpalu

NII AYIKWEI PARKES

Nii Ayikwei Parkes, is a Ghanaian-British producer and writer. A 2007 recipient of Ghana's ACRAG award for poetry, he is Senior Editor at flipped eye publishing and has won acclaim as a children's author, poet, broadcaster and novelist – most notably the Prix Laure Bataillon for the French translation of his novel *Tail of the Blue Bird* (Cape, 2009). Twice featured on London's Poems on the Underground, Nii Ayikwei's ballast series from his début poetry collection *The Makings of You* (Peepal Tree Press, 2010) was described by Ali Smith as "an astonishing, powerful remix of history and language and the possibilities of both". *The Geez* is his second book of poetry.

THE GEEZ

PEEPAL TREE PRESS | £9.99 | PBS PRICE £7.50

The Geez
(pronounced /geɪz/ Gaze)

Nii Ayikwei Parkes

The new form which Parkes has developed, the Gimbal, allows a pivot between, as the poet himself has described it "logic/theory/reason" and "emotion/feeling"; it's an intricate but deftly deployed construction which speaks to the core strength of this collection, a fierce and exuberant language which is always held tightly in control.

The collection contains some beautifully-realised poems of family and parents ("your mother's embrace is a furnace"), or the wonderful poem 'YEAR AD 87: BM14', which salvages from "a world that showers so much terror on skin so dark" the joy and hope of the next generation.

There are also many erotic poems; poems intently focused on the physical, where even the form, such as the use of the "/" in 'BREAK/ABLE' becomes an integral part of the corporeality of the poem. In 'Offside' we get an interesting subversion of the trope of men examining male behaviour with the "I" explaining to his sister about the behaviour of boys – it allows perhaps more honesty and more depth that other similar poems might be able to achieve.

One of the strengths of many of these physical poems is the way they use the bodily experience to act as a hinge, almost like those single lines in the Gimbal form; the poems are both still tethered to a youthful exploration and innocence and yet framed by middle-age.

> The twenty-one year gap in betrayals
> hasn't changed you

That is not to say the poems are held back by this, indeed they keep moving – even in the final lines of the collection: "Some nights my sleep wants / company and it won't settle its vogueing self for less"; that desire for company, that yearning towards other bodies, carries on its journey even after the book ends.

> Thus the body is echo chamber
> and memory; all its parts triggers,
> every bruise history, melody.
>
> I carry all my dreams; not as I imagined,
> but the heft holds – every flower has
> fallen to yield some peculiar fruit.

NII AYIKWEI PARKES

The Geez was born out of the intersection of two things: photography and loss. The primary loss that triggered my reflections was a decision I made in 2014 to walk away from a relationship that was not healthy for me. In rediscovering who I was without that relationship, I started to play at the many things I had let go of. Having moonlighted as a photographer's assistant for a brief period between 1999 and 2000, photography was one of them.

I began to take daily selfies on my phone, constantly deleting and taking new ones, all the while mulling the irony of being seen as a young, happy, party-loving man. What was the world seeing? I was approaching middle-age, feeling empty and wanted nothing more than to be at home hugging my children. Then in 2018, I became acquainted with a photo series by Yagazie Emezi called *The Consumption of the Black Model*, where she had written in the preamble, "Often times... the black body becomes a canvas to project fetishized narratives." It was a statement that clarified my musings, leading me to recognise, in the written work I had produced during my selfie era, a germ that was attempting to amplify that which lies beneath what can be gleaned just by looking – a swallowed whimper that wanted to be loud: "how sharp / that smooth black liquid felt inside me, how hard / these nights that blacken me, broken with grief."

The philosopher Mariana Ortega, who studies aesthetic othering, has written of the way "photography was used... to create hierarchies of being to show dark bodies as deviant and inferior." Once I found this deliberateness in photography I began to look for it everywhere else: could the myth of the crossroads also be a way of diminishing the work and craft Robert Johnson put into developing his unique music? This is where the intersection of music, personal history, race, politics and contemporary culture came together to power *The Geez*.

NII RECOMMENDS

Gabeba Baderoon, *The Dream in the Next Body* (Kwela Books); Alice Walker, *Horses Make a Landscape Look More Beautiful* (Mariner Books); Atukwei Okai, *Logorligi Logarithms* (Ghana Publishing Company); Tracy K. Smith, *The Body's Question* (Graywolf Press); Seamus Heaney, *Electric Light* (Faber); Colette Bryce, *The Full Indian Rope Trick* (Picador); Roger Robinson, *Suckle* (flipped eye); Li-Young Lee, *Rose* (BOA Editions); Amiri Baraka, *Funk Lore* (Littoral Books) and look out for Will Harris, Warsan Shire, Mary Jean Chan, Caleb Femi – lots of exciting early career poets.

RECOMMENDATION

We lose ourselves in the dark edges

A GIMBAL OF BLACKNESS

for Pops

Night cannot grasp the swift flight
of wind, but blackens every tree
the air moves, paints them darker, pushes
them against the light, the shapeless
light that gives them shape to shift

before my eyes. I am often in the embrace

of night; I am myself a dark thing –
the kind that was once called boy when man –
that was born of a woman descended from hills
and a man delivered from boyhood by the sea,

a man now lifeless though he gave me life.

I am often in the embrace of dark thoughts,
in the dim grasp of memory, a bottle in hand,
reflecting the light of the moon. I recall
a can of Guinness left in a London fridge –

one my father bought but didn't get to drink –

kept for me by a well-meaning aunt. And how
hard my throat shrank with every sip, how sharp
that smooth black liquid felt inside me, how hard
these nights that blacken me, broken with grief
for a man I loved, who can no longer grieve.

NII AYIKWEI PARKES

Image: Sophie Davidson

DAISY LAFARGE

Daisy Lafarge grew up in Sussex and South London and has lived in Scotland since 2011. She received an Eric Gregory Award in 2017, and a Betty Trask Award in 2019 for her novel, *Paul*, forthcoming with Granta. Daisy is currently working towards a PhD at the University of Glasgow. *Life Without Air* is her first poetry collection.

LIFE WITHOUT AIR

GRANTA BOOKS | £10.99 | PBS PRICE £8.25

Daisy Lafarge

To encounter Daisy Lafarge's *Life Without Air* is to be plunged into a cosmos radically at odds with itself. We begin with a new day, but not one we recognise:

> I woke up to the grating
> wrack of a mechanical sun,
> it was ticking on its side
> just across the street, spun
> off its great medieval wheels.

Life on earth may be precariously balanced on the fulcrum of our last-ditch Anthropocene moment, but this extends to the Heavens too. Nothing, including the sun or the "too-soon moon", is where it's supposed to be. This is a collection in which things inexplicably disappear (the "opinions" of men with "ideas", for example, who wake to discover themselves "on the wrong side of history"). Into these resonant gaps, Lafarge pitches her restless, philosophical enquiry, suffused with existential anxiety at the end of the Industrial Age:

> ...the world had fallen from its pedestal,
> and in its place left a globular question
> around what has always been.

An entangled mother/daughter relationship is amplified via a wider concern with the poisoning of our own planet, which can no longer mother or sustain us. What we do with our knowledge at this critical juncture becomes the collection's key question ("I am the serrated / dumb knife of I know, I know"). In 'Dredging the Baotou Lake' Lafarge documents the invasion of our hollow Western existences by a man-made lake in Inner Mongolia, poisoned by rare-earth mineral mining, literally brimming with toxicity: "the word meniscus arcs above the table / and crashes over the buzzing lunch-rush / room". Sooner or later, this sequence suggests, we will be forced to connect origin and consequence.

Mercurial, ingenious, and prophetic, this is poetry of and for our off-kilter times. Composed before Covid-19, *Life Without Air* even contains the prescient lines:

> have you ever festered
> in your own quarantine, afraid
> that your toxins would spread?

SINÉAD MORRISSEY

I SELECTOR'S COMMENT

DAISY LAFARGE

The book's title comes from the microbiologist Louis Pasteur, who described the process of fermentation as "la vie sans l'air" – life without air. Before Pasteur's experiments it was believed that the products of the ancient practice of fermentation came about through Spontaneous Generation – the theory that forms of life spring into existence from inert or dead matter. In one of my favourite examples, Aristotle believed that the rare phenomenon of pink snow resulted from the putrefaction of worms (it is actually caused by a type of algae).

Life Without Air includes a selection from my earlier pamphlet *understudies for air* (Sad Press, 2017) and develops its preoccupation with the Pre-Socratic philosopher Anaximenes, who posited air as *arche*, the primary substance from which all things are made. The contemporary philosopher Luce Irigaray retrieves Anaximenes' concerns and accuses Western philosophy of "forgetting" air, the element in which we exist. Irigaray claims that air has been neglected because it "does not show itself", highlighting the centuries-long obsession with what can be seen and verified through the senses of vision and touch.

The collection picks up on the "unseen" nature of air, which figures in the poems both literally and figuratively to explore what "does not show itself", other than by dint of its effects: psychic traumas, interpersonal and ecological wounds and toxicities. Although much of the collection is concerned with human relationships and structures, the book's title is, for me, a way to begin thinking with other forms of life, such as the fermenting bacteria responsible for oxygenating the planet.

DAISY RECOMMENDS

Fanny Howe, *Night Philosophy* (Divided Publishing); Mei-Mei Berssenbrugge, *A Treatise on Stars* (New Directions); Will Alexander, *Compression & Purity* (City Lights); Dom Hale, *Scammer* (87 Press); Bhanu Kapil, *How To Wash A Heart* (Pavilion Poetry); Jazmine Linklater, *Figure a Motion* (Guillemot Press) and Peter Gizzi, *Sky Burial* (Carcanet).

RECOMMENDATION

are you beginning to understand?

FALSIFICATION OF AIR

what can I pass on, you ask,
about methods of detecting the air?
it has become so habitual
I am not sure where to begin.
each morning I walk into the world
looking for signs. early, before light
is normalised by the shadow of buildings
and the gentle fraying of traffic. it seems the signs
are most attracted to states of dereliction.
to receive them, it helps to be empty
but imbued with residual function
like a disused water tower
or any number of withering technologies.
lie back. let the world grow over you
like weeds. consider the sheets of air
gridlocked in double glazing. now
are you beginning to understand?

Image: Ebony Lamb

BILL MANHIRE

Bill Manhire was born in Invercargill, New Zealand in 1946. He was his country's inaugural Poet Laureate and has won the New Zealand Book Award for Poetry four times. He holds a personal chair at the Victoria University of Wellington, where he directs the celebrated creative writing programme and the International Institute of Modern Letters. His volume of short fiction, *South Pacific*, was published by Carcanet in 1994. His poetry collections include *Lifted* (2007), and his *Collected Poems* (2001) and *Selected Poems* (2014).

WOW

CARCANET | £10.99 | PBS PRICE £8.25

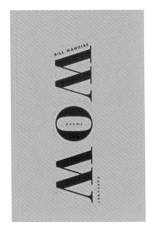

The title *Wow* appears to be both a declaration of amazement and wonder but also one of astonishment, in the sense of being profoundly shocked or scared about the state of the world and what may be to come. In its opening epigraph "they've cleared away / the clearings", pulled from a tweet Manhire wrote back in 2018, and originally entitled 'Loss of Forest', we immediately arrive at the eco-concerns of the collection. The first poem in the voice of the now-extinct Huia bird, ends with a haunting lament:

> I lived among you once
> and now I can't be found
> I'm made of things that vanish
> a feather on the ground

The next poem begins with the ominous: "This book about extinct birds is heavier than any bird"; the weight of what we've lost, and what we are still to lose.

Manhire's skill here, though is to ground these global concerns in the small concrete details of everyday life, the dog's bark that becomes "ice rising out of the sea" is one example of this; the domestic, cosy image of the dog, taking on a grand metaphorical resonance, and yet wearing it lightly.

'Sorrow' perhaps gives us a line with which we can explore the stitching of the rest of the collection: "he says sad is sometimes beautiful"; these are poems which are often gorgeous postcards of a landscape, tinged with impending and already-realised loss. Elsewhere the book offers humour and wit in short bursts of thought and a poet contemplating not only their place in the world, but their place within the self:

> I must be many miles from my own life

In the collection's final poem, 'Little Prayer', Manhire pleads:

> Let there be tasks we undertake
> Let us make what we can make

A world in crisis which demands a very human response.

24   ANDREW McMILLAN

BILL MANHIRE

Wow starts with one bird and ends with another. That may look like careful planning but, like a lot of good things in the world of poetry, is largely accidental.

The book opens with the song of the huia – extinct now for a century – lamenting its own departure from the planet. Ironically its call was voiced by early listeners as uia, uia, uia – where are you? Well, we know where the huia are: there are cabinets full of them in British and European museums. The last piece in *Wow* is a prose poem in which an entirely imaginary bird flies out of a surgical wound, a flight which is – maybe! – hopeful. Prose poem and song. Loss and hopeful moments. Many of my poems stumble around between such possibilities.

There are poems of environmental loss; a rewrite of the Noah story; some unhappy projections into the future. There are also poems about ageing and, as Larkin put it, "the only end of age". In the title poem, a baby says "wow" to life and the astonishing prospect of language, yet almost immediately the world says back to it: Also.

All that said, with most of the poems I had no firm idea what I was writing "about" until I had done the writing. I've always seconded the words sometimes attributed to E.M. Forster: "How do I know what I think till I see what I say?" Bafflement is good for poets. We write to find things out, and if all goes well a poem is there chirping away at the end. My favourite poem definition is Paul Valéry's: "a prolonged hesitation between sound and sense." Poets love that space between music and meaning. That's why we are so often socially inept but keen to sing in front of strangers.

BILL RECOMMENDS

Tusiata Avia, *Wild Dogs Under My Skirt* (Victoria University Press); David Berman, *Actual Air* (Drag City); Jenny Bornholdt, *Lost and Somewhere Else* (VUP); James Brown, *Selected Poems* (VUP); Miles Burrows, *Waiting for the Nightingale* (Carcanet); Janet Frame, *Storms Will Tell* (Bloodaxe); Alison Glenny, *The Farewell Tourist* (Otago University Press); Laura Jensen, *Memory* (Carnegie Mellon); John McAuliffe, *The Kabul Olympics* (Gallery); Christopher Reid, *The Song of Lunch* (CB Editions); Hone Tuwhare, *Small Holes in the Silence* (Vintage).

RECOMMENDATION

HUIA

I was the first of birds to sing
I sang to signal rain
the one I loved was singing
and singing once again

My wings were made of sunlight
my tail was made of frost
my song was now a warning
and now a song of love

I sang upon a postage stamp
I sang upon your coins
but money courted beauty
you could not see the joins

Where are you when you vanish?
Where are you when you're found?
I'm made of greed and anguish
a feather on the ground

+

I lived among you once
and now I can't be found
I'm made of things that vanish
a feather on the ground

AFTER SURGERY

A small bird flies out of the body, out of a blink perhaps, maybe out of the lungs. It wants words for all that's burning. There must be language for the dazzle of its wings, also for what might hold in place a long and lightly feathered scar. The bird contains a thousand possible sounds. It sits on a branch, everywhere-at-once, sharp shadow against the sunset, crumple of gift-wrap on the bed, a throat as yet untuned, practising the names of things it might one day return with. You lift your hand a little, almost to wave. Twig and bandage, says the bird; possibly lilac, possibly rain.

SAFIYA SINCLAIR

Safiya Sinclair was born and raised in Montego Bay, Jamaica. She is the author of *Cannibal*, winner of a Whiting Writers' Award, the OCM Bocas Prize for Caribbean Poetry and the Prairie Schooner Book Prize in Poetry. *Cannibal* was a finalist for the PEN Center USA Literary Award, as well as being longlisted for the PEN Open Book Award and the Dylan Thomas Prize. Sinclair's other honours include a Pushcart Prize, a Ruth Lilly and Dorothy Sargent Rosenberg Fellowship. Her work has appeared in *The New Yorker, Granta, The Nation*, and elsewhere. She received her MFA in poetry at the University of Virginia, and is currently a PhD candidate in literature and creative writing at the University of Southern California.

RECOMMENDATION

CANNIBAL

PICADOR | £10.99 | PBS PRICE £8.25

In 'Elocution Lessons with Ms Silverstone' the speaker asserts:

Let's call you mirage.
As if you were possible.
As if you could invent your place. Rasta-girl, interloper. Whatever.

And this is exactly what Safiya Sinclair has achieved in *Cannibal*: a language forged afresh in order to refashion a home out of multiple forms of elision, dispossession and exile. "At a very young age I identified with Caliban as a representative of the linguistic and psychological exile of the Caribbean self", Sinclair explains in an interview for *The Rumpus*, and *The Tempest* is used as inspiration and structuring device, the play's five acts mirrored in *Cannibal's* five discreet sections, each prefaced with a quotation by or about Caliban. In 'Dreaming in Foreign' she urges:

Give your throat to everything,
not the word but the thing of it.
What the body speaks is untranslatable.

In 'Pocomania' the word "father" is used as noun, verb, punctuation mark and direct addressee – rolled over and re-invented in Sinclair's looping syntax:

Father washing me in eucalyptus, in garlic, in goldenseal.
Fathering my exorcism. Father the harsh brine of my sea.

Elsewhere she takes racist propaganda in the form of pseudo-scientific tracts such as *100 Amazing Facts About the Negro, with Complete Proof* (1934) and turns its language against itself, deftly creating a self-detonating text: "Do not / attempt to understand the diction of a Negro; / he wakes in strange tongues and speaks entirely / with his body." Sinclair exposes the proximity of slavery, documenting the discovery of slave quarters in student dorms at the University of Virginia ("Somewhere, the ghost arm of history / still throttling me. The taste of old blood on the wind"). Ghosts are everywhere, and the act of being haunted/hunted is an immediate and continual threat. To read *Cannibal* is to "breath[e]" "the dark impossible", to enter a reconfigured luminous imaginary where "nothing grows politely".

SINÉAD MORRISSEY

I SELECTOR'S COMMENT

SAFIYA SINCLAIR

Here I am, in a hurricane. Still finding music in its fury. As a matter of survival, most of us born in the Caribbean navigate the strange violence of writing in the language of the colonist, the language of our oppression. "We are all strangers here," Derek Walcott said of our dual identity, "our bodies think in one language and move in another." As a Jamaican poet, I've had to make a distinction of which tongue? Which self? Do I express my thoughts through the wild, brazen drama of patois, or navigate the margins of English prosody?

Cannibal explores Jamaican womanhood as a locus of this exile, while aiming to decolonise English and its imperial terror. By interrogating *The Tempest* and other colonial texts through an anticolonial lens, each poem is rooted in Kamau Brathwaite's idea that "The hurricane does not roar in pentameters." I wanted each poem to mirror the fertile landscape of Jamaica, the hunger of the sea's crashing and sage whispering. Our verdant hills and bursting blooms, our hissing vines and heavy fruit trees. Here on the page, as in the tropics, nothing grows politely. Many of these poems are sung through the throat of Caliban, reflecting a poetry of the impolite body. Like Caliban, I aim to startle and disrupt, to conjure hurricanes: "You taught me your language; and my profit on't / Is I know how to curse."

Always in my ear is the insurgence of Jamaica's linguistic tradition – the fevered tempo of our dialect, the fire-root of reggae's one-drop, our matriarchal folklore, its immutable song. I wrote *Cannibal* not only to reframe the historical wounds of my island, but to build a home against my inherited homelessness. A wilful remaking of the cannibal self. What was once seen as savage, I celebrate as mine. Poetry as reclamation. Poetry as survival.

SAFIYA RECOMMENDS

Natalie Diaz, *Postcolonial Love Poem* (Faber); Rachel Eliza Griffiths, *Seeing the Body* (W.W. Norton); Aria Aber, *Hard Damage* (University of Nebraska Press); francine j. harris, *Here is the Sweet Hand* (FSG); Bettina Judd, *Patient* (Black Lawrence Press); Nicole Sealey, *Ordinary Beast* (Ecco); Ladan Osman, *Exiles of Eden* (Coffee House Press); Aracelis Girmay, *Kingdom Animalia* (BOA Editions); Shara McCallum, *Madwoman* (Alice James Books); Shivanee Ramlochan, *Everyone Knows I Am a Haunting* (Peepal Tree Press) and Rachel Long, *My Darling from the Lions* (Picador).

know I too am scorching there.
Igniting and devouring

Image: Firelei Báez

AUTOBIOGRAPHY

When I was a child
I counted the looper moths
caught in the dusty mesh
of our window screens.

Fed them slowly into the hot mouth
of a kerosene lamp, then watched
them pop and blacken soundlessly,
but could not look away.

I had known what it was to be nothing.
Bore the shamed blood-letter of my sex
like a banishment; wore the bruisemark
of my father's hands to school in silence.

And here I am, still at the old window
dying of thirst, watching my girlself asleep
with the candle flame alive in my ear,
little sister yelling *fire!*

STAYING HUMAN ANTHOLOGY

BLOODAXE BOOKS | £12.99 | PBS PRICE £9.75

new poems for *Staying Alive*
edited by NEIL ASTLEY

Staying Human has landed: the fourth iteration of Bloodaxe's "real poems for unreal times" anthology series, which began in 2002 with *Staying Alive* – a publishing phenomenon which introduced thousands of new readers to poetry. Once again, here are five hundred poems, divided into categories both wide-ranging ("Ten Zillion Things") and quirkily specific ("After Frank O'Hara"). But the joy of the endeavour remains the same: a cacophony of voices, some new, some familiar, some canonical, some recently published, threaded together into an urgent and moving conversation about what it means to be human, alive, and enmeshed in our own mortality and in our relationships with other people.

The trademark strengths of Bloodaxe are fully reflected here: a genuinely open conception of what poetry is, who it is for and what it can achieve; a commitment to diverse representation, particularly in terms of publishing women and poets of colour; and an international focus not shy of offering poetry in translation on an equal footing with English-language poetry.

Poets respond to life, but they also respond to other poems. The editor Neil Astley speaks of "orchestrating" his selections so as to bring this enabling dialogue between poets – most overt in the Frank O'Hara section but present throughout – alive for readers. What is equally striking is the range of poetry Astley has drawn on; his choices indicative (naturally enough) of his personal enthusiasms and encyclopaedic knowledge of the art form.

The two final sections (Empathy and Conflict and The Future?) resoundingly illustrate poetry's power in "uncertain times". Assembled in a Spring marked by the double crises of Covid-19 and the police killing of George Floyd, poem after poem stands out as vital and incisive – hewn testimonies to injustice we cannot live without. Buy this book. Buy it for your friends. It's a present to last a lifetime.

> It means once in a lifetime
> That justice can rise up
> And hope and history rhyme.
> - Seamus Heaney

SINÉAD MORRISSEY

CARVING BY IMTIAZ DHARKER

Others can carve out
their space
in tombs and pyramids.
Our time cannot be trapped
in cages.
Nor hope, nor laughter.
We let the moment rise
like birds and planes and angels
to the sky.
Eternity is this.
Your breath on the window-pane,
living walls with shining eyes.
The surprise of spires,
uncompromising verticals. Knowing
we have been spared
to lift our faces up
for one more day,
into one more sunrise.

THE DAY LAID BARE
KIWAO NOMURA, TRANSLATED BY ERIC SELLAND
ISOBAR PRESS | £10.00 | PBS PRICE £7.50

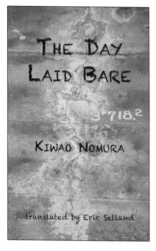

Ma, or "negative space," is an important concept in traditional Japanese arts from the Noh drama to brush painting, meaning the pause or moment of silence in drama and the empty space in painting, becomes an active space. This traditional use of negation is important to keep in mind when reading *The Day Laid Bare* by Kiwao Nomura, beautifully translated from Japanese by Eric Selland. A cinematic, striking collection, this is a book-long sequence that begins with negation, quoting European modernist Gherasim Luca: "There is no place left in this world for poets." But negation, for Nomura, is where the lyric originates: "When disquiet / with its one hundred legs / puts down roots all around me."

For some readers, this poetics might evoke early modernist cinema: absurdist, humorous, highly experimental, the lyric fragmentation here is a part of the narrative structure, so distant music ("music I heard coming from somewhere in the bone") enters at the most unexpected, strangest, shivering moments – and stays. Yet, a moment comes in this interplay of lyric fragments and spaces, when all the technical bravura falls off, when crisis happens, what do we see? "Without crisis," Nomura once wrote, "there would be no modern Japanese poetry." And so we see a poet searching for "the flesh of voice," we see an attempt to understand something beyond words: "stripped to the bone / the day laid bare".

THE POET & TRANSLATOR

Kiwao Nomura was born in 1953 and is a leading experimental voice in contemporary Japanese poetry. He is also a major critic and theorist, who, along with Shuri Kido, provided a new interpretation of Japan's postwar period in literature. He has published twenty-six volumes of poetry since 1987, written on French poets, including Rimbaud, and translated the complete poems of René Char into Japanese. In September 2020 he was awarded the 38th Modern Poetry Prize by the Japan Poets Association for his collection *Twilight Saudade*.

Eric Selland has translated Japanese literature for almost forty years. He has published two poetry books *Arc Tangent* (Isobar Press) and *Object States* (Theenk Books) and translated the bestselling novel, *The Guest Cat* by Takashi Hiraide.

ILYA KAMINSKY

I SELECTOR'S COMMENT

ROADBLOCK10
(SHADOW OF FLESH)

You, shined on by sun, and above
Shadow of flesh swaying
It is myself...
What have I become?
A shadow wandering
Expanding, contracting
Changing shape like an amoeba
Swaying back and forth
Yes, it's me
An old song wafts in on the breeze
Might be Lenny Kravitz
'Are You Gonna Go My Way?'
More and more the shadow moves
Dances to the beat of the music
But it is not having fun
Simply becomes more and more the shadow
The shadow which
Above you, on whom the sun shines,
Begins to go mad, as if flipping to the beat
Heading in no direction, resembling a prayer
It is myself
Shined on by never-ending sun
Floating endlessly above you

TRANSLATION CHOICE

37

THE ABDUCTION
MARAM AL-MASRI, TRANSLATED BY THEO DORGAN
SOUTHWORD | £9.99 | PBS PRICE £7.50

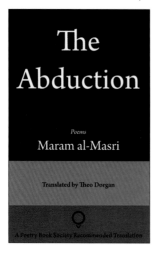

Maram al-Masri's tenth book, deftly translated by Theo Dorgan, is an endlessly moving and compelling book about a mother's grief, written when the speaker's estranged husband abducts their infant child. With clarity and emotional intensity, al-Masri explores the landscape and various shapes of grief. "Come on, sun, wake up!" the poet begins, "I mean to take my child for a walk," and we observe the first steps:

> I pick you up and I hum
> you walk, hesitant,
> like a duck.
> You fall and you pick yourself up,
> we try again
> fall, get up again.
>
> It is like this,
> life,
> my little urchin;
> before we can become
> horses, galloping.

The little joys of early parenthood are on full display here: "I talk to him / as to a friend... / All this time, he is occupied with taking / the spoons out of the drawer." And, soon, the disaster happens: "I had a child / I hid him in my belly / he shared my body... // he was torn from my arms / I ceased to sing." Yet, sing she does:

> There is war in Rwanda
> and me, I am dining.
> There is war in Yugoslavia
> and me, I am smiling.
> There is war in Palestine
> and me, I am asleep.
> Since you were taken
> the war is in me.

THE POET & TRANSLATOR

Maram al-Masri was born in Syria and has lived in France since 1982. She has published numerous collections, including *Liberty Walks Naked,* translated by Theo Dorgan, whose own collections include *Nine Bright Shiners* and *Orpheus.*

ILYA KAMINSKY

SELECTOR'S COMMENT

THE BREAD OF LETTERS
II.

The act of writing,
is it not a scandalous act in itself?

To write,
it is learning to know oneself in the most intimate thoughts

Yes I am scandalous
because I point to my truth and my nakedness as a woman,

yes I am scandalous
because I cry my sorrow and my hope
my desire, my hunger and my thirst.

To write
is to describe the multiple faces of man
the beautiful and the ugly
the tender and the cruel.

To write is to die in front of a person
upon whom you look, unmoved,

it is to drown in sight of a boat that passes close
without seeing you.

To write
is to be the boat that will save
the drowning.

To write
is to live on a cliff's edge
clinging to a blade
of grass.

Image: Louie Mire

WILLIAM GEE

William Gee is a poet and writer based in East London. His work often focuses on chronic illness, trauma, and the intersectionality between the two. He won a Bare Fiction prize for poetry, and a Troubadour Prize, and was published in *Bare Fiction*, *Rising*, *Roulade* and *Proletarian Poetry*. His debut pamphlet, *Rheuma*, was published with Bad Betty Press in 2020.

RHEUMA BY WILLIAM GEE

BAD   BETTY   PRESS | £6.00 |

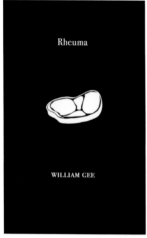

Rheuma

WILLIAM GEE

Rheuma by William Gee is an assured pamphlet which vividly explores the poet's experiences of living with fibromyalgia, a condition that results in chronic pain. Gee depicts the male body's vulnerabilities through fragmented, unpunctuated verse that often leaves the reader feeling breathless, as if to mimic the ways in which the speaker tells himself to:

> breathe but not too much you're about to mistake
> your stomach
> for your lungs swallow until your gut is breathing
> this is the part where you start to feel sick your
> insides threatening
> mate are you ok...

The anxious and self-conscious tone which inhabits these poems draws attention to how chronic illness is too often deemed unacceptable in a capitalist society that rewards the appearance of self-sufficiency, as the speaker in 'self talk' reminds himself to "smile even though you don't have any reason to smile / you just want to look normal and normal people smile". There is a pervasive fear of disappointing others, ranging from one's colleagues to one's mother:

> I'm sorry mum   let me keep this mouth-
> ful forever let nothing come up
> let me keep this mouth
> full all I can taste is love I am soaked
> in it...

Other poems illustrate the impact of childhood trauma on the speaker's mental health with visceral immediacy:

> twenty three now and still I keep my head blank
> in case when accidentally my hand is touched
> greencarpetbedroomfloor
> and all my boy memories
> lie down

In a poetic style reminiscent of work by Wayne Holloway-Smith, Richard Scott and Andrew McMillan, Gee writes with an urgency which demands that we listen. This pamphlet offers a world suffused with pain, yearning and beauty, as the poet writes tenderly of the multitudes he contains.

I SELECTOR'S COMMENT

NICK MAKOHA & MARY JEAN CHAN

TELL ME ANYTHING

for Will

sit down who you love and tell them
and tell them everything I promise
nothing changes after except sometimes the phone
doesn't ring when you shift your whole self
over it over and over I count
things that won't open again
literally make a list
the names that mouths belong to
the types of fist
my hands around the soft bits of my most difficult body
naked in that summer's bedroom the violence
I am holding was put in my lap
   was taken

MATTHEW SWEENEY

Matthew Sweeney (1952-2018) was born in Lifford, Co. Donegal, Ireland, and lived in London from 1973 until the late 90s. After living in Berlin and Timisoara for some years, he returned to Ireland and settled in Cork. He died in August 2018 from motor neurone disease. His books include two collections from Secker, five from Cape, and four from Bloodaxe: *Horse Music* (2013), *Inquisition Lane* (2015), *My Life as a Painter* (2018) and the posthumous *Shadow of the Owl* (2020). *Black Moon* (Cape, 2007) was shortlisted for the T.S. Eliot Prize. *Horse Music* was a Poetry Book Society Recommendation and won the inaugural Pigott Poetry Prize in association with Listowel Writers' Week.

SHADOW OF THE OWL

BLOODAXE BOOKS | £10.99 | PBS PRICE £8.25

MATTHEW SWEENEY

I want to stay off that train as long as I can, despite
all the exhortations to board now.
I want to be myself till the last minute.

In the poem 'The Tube' Matthew Sweeney's closing tercet encapsulates so much of what his innovative and posthumous collection *Shadow of the Owl* is working around. Sweeney was diagnosed with motor neuron disease in late autumn 2017; ten months later he died. The poems in the collection, written from the point of his diagnosis, confront a life unfairly curtailed. In the opening sequence entitled 'The Owl', Sweeney reckons with the impermanence of being, by way of a symbolic meditation through which he eventually reconciles himself to his fate.

Sweeney's owl, an omnipotent and mercurial symbol, is depicted at times as menacing and at others as a companion.

Where does the owl go during the day?
How can he know I'll still be here
when he surfaces?

As poems develop one feels a sense of a life rapidly on the verge of expiration. Often there is a persistence in the speaker's sense of trepidation, situating the poems in a helpless midpoint overseen by a rising uncertainty:

I'm not asking for a map, but I'd like to know
where I'm headed, if not where I'll end up.
And I'd like to know it as soon as I can.

Elsewhere Sweeney incorporates some brighter detailing – small bucolic gardens and riverbanks offset the book's more macabre moments. Memories are evoked, train rides and aeroplanes allude to a zest for life. Despite the tragic subject matter Sweeney refuses sentimentality, at least explicitly, calling instead on his much-celebrated humour and unfettered imagination, which throughout his life, won him the affection of so many readers. A poet of great wit and invention who'll be deeply missed by so many of us.

ANTHONY ANAXAGOROU

1.

No one knows where I'm going,
not even me. Although that owl
I heard outside last night might
lead me to the terrain and call out
the custodians so they can
surround and welcome me, or
do whatever they want to do. I won't
speak, won't say my name even if
they try to coerce me, or play
unearthly music, such as sailors
hear far out on the Atlantic, in fog
so thick they venture to climb it
to reach clear sky. Some do and speak
of large blue birds that glide there
silently as ghosts, but those men
return too damaged to speak much
or stay above ground very long.
The owl could tell more, if he wanted
but he won't. And not only that,
he's decided he will never be seen.

WINTER BOOK REVIEWS

MARGARET ATWOOD: DEARLY

The first collection in over a decade by the Booker Prize winner Margaret Atwood. With characteristic wit and empathy, Atwood turns her attention to ageing, "these are the late poems. / Most poems are late / of course", and looks back on "time laid out like a picnic / in the sun". But these poems look to the future too in carefully crafted micro dystopia which urge positive change, "turn up the light: sing on, / sing: On." Both ecological, playful and political, this is the perfect Christmas gift for Atwood fans to treasure.

NOVEMBER | CHATTO | £14.99 | PBS PRICE £11.25

EAVAN BOLAND: THE HISTORIANS

A moving final volume from one of the most masterful poets of the twentieth century who sadly passed away earlier this year. Over her almost sixty-year career, Eavan Boland remained a vital voice in feminist and Irish literature. *The Historians* presents Boland at the height of her powers, giving voice to the often overlooked lives of ordinary women. This is a fitting tribute to a poet whose work has revised history as we know it and whose talent will be much missed.

OCTOBER | CARCANET | £10.99 | PBS PRICE £8.25

TED HUGHES: CROW ANNIVERSARY EDITION

This hardback anniversary edition celebrates fifty years since the publication of Ted Hughes' 1970 masterpiece, *Crow*. Re-issued with a new foreword by Marina Warner which explores *Crow's* iconic status and contextualises the influence of ancient legends on the creation of this "hulking, metamorphic beast-bird". A timely revival, this modern myth takes on new significance in our own age of uncertainty, where the primordial struggles between light and dark feel more visceral and urgent than ever.

OCTOBER | FABER | £14.99 (HB) | PBS PRICE £11.25

INUA ELLAMS: THE ACTUAL

Born in Nigeria, Inua Ellams is a poet, playwright and rising star to watch. *The Actual* unleashes its fierce, expletive energy, with urgency and fury, on everything from injustice to racism and toxic masculinity. Each of these fifty-five poems begins with F*** in a fast paced, staccato sequence of raw musicality and mastery. These poems look us squarely in the eye and ask, "What the actual—?" Their rage is deep seated, palpable and vital.

OCT | PENNED IN THE MARGINS | £9.99 | PBS PRICE £7.50

CALEB FEMI: POOR

Raised on the North Peckham estate where Damilola Taylor was murdered, Caleb Femi exposes "what it feels like to be Black here: like you're dead & alive at the same time". *Poor* reveals the reality of gentrification, "hipsters take selfies / on the corners where our / friends died, the rent goes up", and institutional racism, stopped and searched aged thirteen "you fit / the description", but Femi digs beneath these shocking headlines to the lived experience and demands, "what do you know about this story – the full of it?"

NOVEMBER | PENGUIN | £9.99 | PBS PRICE £7.50

ROSIE GARLAND: WHAT GIRLS DO IN THE DARK

An enthralling collection, *What Girls Do in the Dark* is at once concerned with the inhuman scale of stars and astronomical events and the human scale of individual lives, effortlessly inter-twining the epic nature of the galaxy with the subjective quality of the here-and-now. This is something of a magic trick, and reading this collection is akin to listening to a magician subtly explaining how their acts work, through association, transformation, and wonderful appeals to the imagination.

OCTOBER | NINE ARCHES PRESS | £9.99 | PBS PRICE £7.50

BOOK REVIEWS

WINTER BOOK REVIEWS

CLIVE JAMES: THE FIRE OF JOY

James completed this selection of "roughly eighty poems to get by heart and say aloud" shortly before he passed away last year, and *The Fire of Joy* is a fitting testament to a life suffused with poetry, anthologising a treasure trove of the celebrated poet's favourite works by other writers across centuries of literature. Each poem comes with commentary both on the work and James' relationship with it, and so *The Fire of Joy* becomes both an autobiography filled with humour and insight, as well as a wonderful poetic resource.

OCTOBER | PICADOR | £20.00 HB | PBS PRICE £15.00

ANDREW MOTION: RANDOMLY MOVING PARTICLES

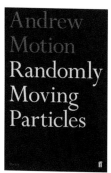

This darkly compelling collection by the former Poet Laureate is a profound examination of how a universe based on "randomly moving particles" can create systems and spectacles epic in scope and deeply complex in structure. From the awesome scale of geological time and astronomical distance, to the chilling depths of human psychology, this collection contains powerful sequences of poetic vigour which transport the reader across vast reaches of time, space and experience.

OCTOBER | FABER | £14.99 | PBS PRICE £11.25

ADNAN AL SAYEGH, TRANS. JENNY LEWIS: LET ME TELL YOU WHAT I SAW

Jenny Lewis and Ruba Abughaida present bilingual extracts from Al-Sayegh's *Uruk's Anthem*, one of the longest poetic works of Arabic literature. During the time of composition, Al-Sayegh was forcibly conscripted into the Iran-Iraq war. *Uruk's Anthem* is therefore steeped in the tragic history of Iraq, but is a work of beauty, as much as tragedy. Epic in scope, lyrical and deeply moving, this is a fascinating and powerful work, and a welcome addition to the canon of translated poetry.

OCTOBER | SEREN | £12.99 | PBS PRICE £9.75

ARUNDHATHI SUBRAMANIAM: LOVE WITHOUT A STORY

Subramaniam's verse is imbued with the spiritual and mythic in this wonderful collection, *Love Without A Story*. Poised and measured, these poems encourage the reader to think and feel deeply, to sit and watch as Subramaniam unveils artfully composed observations about the cosmos we inhabit and those we share it with. *Love Without a Story* is a breath-taking and heart-warming collection.

NOVEMBER | BLOODAXE | £10.99 | PBS PRICE £8.25

NGŨGĨ WA THIONG'O: THE PERFECT NINE

Translated by the author into English, *The Perfect Nine* presents an epic origin story of the Kenyan *Gĩkũyũ* people. *The Perfect Nine* refers to nine original matriarchs who founded their nation, and who Thiong'o describes as "the original feminists." Here is a mythological and metaphysical feast, bursting with sensory verse and dropping the reader into a rich world oozing colour and adventure. In parts *The Perfect Nine* seems to be a sacred text, dazzling in its eloquence.

OCTOBER | PENGUIN | £12.00 | PBS PRICE £9.00

CHRISTMAS PRESENTS: TEN POEMS TO GIVE AND RECEIVE

Christmas wouldn't be complete without a beautiful new Candlestick press anthology and this year is no exception. *Christmas Presents* unwraps ten entertaining poems to give and receive this festive season. Full of the magic of Christmas, this mini anthology includes poems by Andre Bagoo, Ben Wilkinson, Helen Ivory and John Greening. Intricately illustrated by Sarah Young, this delightful gift includes a bookmark and an envelope, making it a thoughtful alternative to a Christmas card.

CANDLESTICK PRESS | £4.95

WINTER PAMPHLETS

UZMAH ALI: BREATHE BEFORE THOUGHT

There is a near-ethereal quality to Ali's verse, which even when speaking to long histories of cultural oppression retains a calm wisdom, delivering concise, unmitigated truths. This is a collection about belonging and identity, about the complex relationships individuals hold to different places, as well as the inter-relation between how we are seen and how we see ourselves. Ali navigates the landscapes of Wales, London and Lahore, and the social, political and cultural lenses through which landscapes are experienced, with an artistic grace.

WATERLOO   PRESS | £8.00 |

A.K. BLAKEMORE: SHIA LA BEOUF

"i harbour a real affection for Shia", writes Blakemore in the titular poem, which is an appropriate summary for the pamphlet as a whole. Blakemore treats LaBeouf with a humanising tenderness, which is perhaps unusual when addressing such an outwardly strange creature as a celebrity. Blakemore's intimate evocative poems impress as exercises in breaking down facades of otherness and rendering experiences with a palpable relatability. This is a pamphlet which demands, and rewards, attention.

MAKINA   BOOKS | £7.00 |

HELEN CALCUTT: SOMEHOW

A heart-breaking elegy for the poet's own brother Matthew who committed suicide. Alongside this devastating loss, sit poems about motherhood, sex and the bodily weight of grief. *Somehow* captures the impossibility of explaining death to a young child, "she asks me how he died. / he was very sad, I say / and she seems to understand", and the dehumanising effect of a coroner's report: "there is nothing / significant about / the deceased". These are poems of deep compassion and loss which culminate in quiet observations of the world, a new appreciation of life.

VERVE   PRESS | £7.50 |

DAVID MILLER: VITRUVIAN SHADOWS

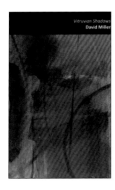

Reading this captivating limited-edition pamphlet is somewhat akin to hearing mingled echoes of conversation within a mysterious underground place. Elusive and tantalising, Miller recalls Joyce and borrows snippets from Vitruvius' *The Ten Books on Architecture* to create an evocative and mysterious short sequence. *Vitruvian Shadows* is built from elements of space and architecture, fragments of the psyche, and a pervading darkness shot through with flashes of keen descriptive power.

RED CEILINGS PRESS | £6.00 |

JAZMINE LINKLATER: FIGURE A MOTION

Inspired by exhibitions at the Castlefield art gallery, here we become the art object: "See how here at the edge of the object / it isn't the end but the seam where you join". Linklater's poems "speak us / to proximity" in an experimental ekphrasis. *Figure a Motion* holds an elusive strength or "in-stability" in which words are "at once whole and fragmented". Nowhere more so than in 'Pulse Pulse', a concentric poem which urges us to look again at the art of looking. This is electrifying stuff; a fluid "prismatic knowing".

GUILLEMOT PRESS | £6.00 |

ARIADNE RADI COR: L'ITALIE L'ONDON

This dual language Italian-English pamphlet is enriched by found objects and the ephemera of interior life. Radi Cor interweaves memories of Italy, "under the blue-painted days of summer", with life in London, embodying the two: "The partition between the continents is on my rib cage". Belonging is a double state of being and "We have to behave like roots, be invisible / and hold the world together." This pamphlet will resonate with all those still searching for their place in the world.

KNIVES FORKS SPOONS | £10.00 |

PAMPHLET REVIEWS

WINTER BOOK LISTINGS

AUTHOR	TITLE	PUBLISHER	RRP
Bebe Ashley	Gold Light Shining	Banshee Lit	£10.00
Ed. Neil Astley	Staying Human	Bloodaxe Books	£12.99
Margaret Atwood	Dearly	Chatto & Windus	£14.99
Nii Ayikwei Parkes	The Geez	Peepal Tree Press	£9.99
John Birtwhistle	In The Event	Carcanet Press	£12.99
Eavan Boland	The Historians	Carcanet Press	£10.99
Anthony Burgess	Collected Poems	Carcanet Press	£25.00
Anne Caldwell	Alice and the North	Valley Press	£9.99
Thomas A. Clark	The Threadbare Coat: Selected Poems	Carcanet Press	£12.99
David Constantine	Belongings	Bloodaxe Books	£10.99
Fred D'Aguiar	Letters to America	Carcanet Press	£10.99
T.S. Eliot	Murder in the Cathedral (Anniversary edition)	Faber & Faber	£9.99
Inua Ellams	The Actual	Penned in the Margins	£9.99
R.F. Francis	Subsidence	Smokestack Books	£7.99
Wendy French	Bread without Butter : Bara heb fenyn	Rockingham Press	£9.99
John Fuller	Asleep and Awake	Chatto & Windus	£12.00
Graham Fulton	Chips, Paracetamol and Wine	Smokestack Books	£7.99
Rosie Garland	What Girls Do in the Dark	Nine Arches Press	£9.99
Alan Gillis	The Readiness	Pan Macmillan	£10.99
John Glenday	Selected Poems	Pan Macmillan	£14.99
John Greening & Stuart Henson	A Postcard to	Red Squirrel Press	£10.00
Caroline Hardaker	Little Quakes Every Day	Valley Press	£10.99
Kerry Hardie	Where Now Begins	Bloodaxe Books	£9.95
Matthew Hedley Stoppard	The Garland King	Valley Press	£9.99
W N Herbert	The Wreck of the Fathership	Bloodaxe Books	£12.99
Ted Hughes	Crow (50th anniversary edition)	Faber & Faber	£12.99
Clive James	The Fire Of Joy	Pan Macmillan	£20.00
Ed. Anna Johnson	Chaos: Poetry Anthology	Patrician Press	£9.00
Tess Jolly	Breakfast at the Origami Café	Blue Diode Publishing	£10.00
Adam Kammerling	Seder	Out-Spoken Press	£10.00
Ed. James Keery	Apocalypse: An Anthology	Carcanet Press	£19.99
Daisy Lafarge	Life Without Air	Granta	£10.99
Julia Rose Lewis	High Erratic Ecology	Knives Forks Spoons	£10.00
Bill Manhire	Wow	Carcanet Press	£10.99
Andrew Motion	Randomly Moving Particles	Faber & Faber	£14.99
Catherine Okoronkwo	Blood and Water	Waterloo Press	£12.00
Ann Pasternak Slater	The Fall of a Sparrow: Vivien Eliot's Life...	Faber & Faber	£35.00
Leeanne Quinn	Some Lives	Dedalus Press	£11.00
Gita Ralleigh	A Terrible Thing	Bad Betty Press	£8.00
Ricky Ray	The Sound of the Earth Singing To Herself	Fly on the Wall Press	£6.99
Christopher Reid	The Late Sun	Faber & Faber	£14.99
Robin Robertson	Grimoire	Pan Macmillan	£14.99
Maurice Scully	Things That Happen	Shearsman Books	£9.95
Safiya Sinclair	Cannibal	Pan Macmillan	£10.99
Rachel Smith	Read(writ)ing Words	Penteract Press	£9.00
Arundhathi Subramaniam	Love Without a Story	Bloodaxe Books	£10.99
Matthew Sweeney	Shadow of the Owl	Bloodaxe Books	£10.99
Sheila Templeton	Clyack	Red Squirrel Press	£10.00
Claudine Toutoungi	Two Tongues	Carcanet Press	£10.99
George Ttoouli	from Animal Illicit	Broken Sleep Books	£8.99
Various	Myth & Metamorphosis	Penteract Press	£10.00
Michael Vince	The Long Distance	Mica Press	£8.99
Andrea Witzke Slot	The Ministry of Flowers	Valley Press	£12.00